For Helen —

hope you enjoy this story and especially the photography! Happy Christmas —

love from Pat & Harry.

A Knopf Book
published by
Random House Australia Pty Ltd
20 Alfred Street, Milsons Point, NSW 2061
http://www.randomhouse.com.au

Sydney   New York Toronto
London Auckland Johannesburg
and agencies throughout the world

First published by Random House Australia in 1997

National Library of Australia
Cataloguing-in-Publication Data:

Mears, Gillian.
Paradise is a place.
ISBN 0 09 183641 7.
I. Edwards, Sandy. II. Title.
A823.3

Design by Yolande Gray
Typeset by Yolande Gray
Printed by Southbank Book

10 9 8 7 6 5 4 3 2 1

Acknowledgement is due for permission to
reprint the lines on page 7 ('The Golden
Builders XXVI' by Vincent Buckley in *Selected
Poems*, published by HarperCollins);
page 8 ('Elegy for Drowned Children' by
Bruce Dawe in *Sometimes Gladness: Collected
Poems, 1954–1992*, published by Addison
Wesley Longman Australia); and pages 57–58
(haiku by Basho in Jack Kornfield's *A Path
With Heart*, published by Bantam Books).

PARADISE IS A PLACE
GILLIAN MEARS AND SANDY EDWARDS

KNOPF

When I am five or six he carries me through the waves on his shoulders. Daddy is his name, or Daddy Peter, so that in my mind he's always connected to daddy-long-legs, the fragile spiders near the top of the tentpoles. Or as he breasts a wave, I imagine he is the seahorse of my mother's stories and that on his back I'll reach the other side of the world.

'Gillian,' he says, trying to loosen my grip around his throat. 'You have to let me breathe. Hold onto my hair. Hold on.'

For the moment I have no need of legs. As the waves begin to splash higher I tighten my fingers around two clumps of his mane. His curls are not wild at all but tight and sculptural, with a hint of blue inside their blackness against a blue sky.

My hair is the colour of the beetle after which I am nicknamed, that comes in the evenings to sit on my hand and double-syllabically click to me if I try to stroke his narrow brown wing cases. Even many years after the names Nipsy, Nipsle, Nipsy Beetle have slid from family

usage, the beetle still flies in an open window across the light near my desk. No one calls me those names anymore and no one ever will again, but to remember them brings to me a knowledge of how tenderly I was loved by my parents.

How fragile and funny I seem to them at the age of five. I have the antics and shyness of an insect and if ever I cry at the Goonellabah house, my father piggybacks me to a long-lived black spider at the edge of the verandah. Mopsy Spider's her name and I must watch her until my tears are dry.

'Stand on my shoulders, Nipsy,' says my father, holding out my arms horizontal to the sea. Perhaps he too wants my mother's gaze. His back is slippery but he leans forward so that by gripping with my toes I can stand up. Now there is a lot more air about me and the sea is so far below that except for my father's voice I would be afraid. My father begins to walk towards the shore and the closer we get, the taller I grow. I am nearly as tall as the headland. I can see our tent top and the seven black cockatoos screaming in a black wave across the tree line, my mother waving and clouds like a baby has just crawled quickly out of a sack of flour and across the sky. Then it is the sea's silver pelt reclaiming my attention as my father swings me once, twice, and then I am in the water. I am in and foaming with a happiness so great it has to come out of me in a sequence of snorts and screams, which are met by the noises of my sisters desperate for their turn to go out into the waves on his shoulders.

The days are full of games. One follows another and favourites which prevail one summer fall from popularity the next. We play leap-frog, stuck-in-the-mud, chasies with Bar the pandanus tree trunk, red-rover-cross-over. All the time the children must egg on the grown-ups. At first they seem to have forgotten how to run and throw, or they begin only in the most half-hearted of ways, but these old skills can make an unexpected return, lighting up a mother's or a father's face to show us that our persistence was worthwhile after all. For a hot and sweaty parent to be run into the sea by their children is happiness enough to make them yell like the girl or the boy they must have once been, as the first wave bursts over their middles.

ONE MORE DAY OF MY LIFE WAS DYING, I think years later at the same beach, but so much older now that the niece who is possibly the most like me lets out an exclamation that sounds almost like fear, because the sunburn has deepened the lines around my mouth. How strange seem my large teeth, she says. Sort of monsterish, she tells me, reluctant yet compelled to convey this unpleasant information. I think how fleeting are the years between when being burnt brings out all the beauty of bones and when it emphasises the age of thinning skin.

The frank, unintentionally harsh observational power of children is never more apparent than in the company of my eldest niece. She has long fine hair and as she rises up through a wave reminds me of nothing so much as the colour plate of the little mermaid in the old Hans Christian Andersen edition from our childhood. Even in the sea she's not entirely relaxed, cocking a critical eye over her old pair of swimmers.

The cool rang through every nerve and surface. I float in the water the way my father once did, watching a nephew, the little Taurean one, who still cannot swim very well but rather uses his head like a determined and bobbing cork. I call out to him, angry with myself. If only I were a much better aunt, I think, I would find the time to take the children to swimming classes. I turn to make a rapid count of nephews and nieces. The oldest ones are body-surfing towards me with maniacal, wave-filled grins. I say to the smaller nephew that if ever he's swept out to sea, rather than attempting to swim against the rip, he must simply float on his back until a boat or a mother or an aunt comes to his rescue.

Last week a boy the age of one of my nephews drowned in the river. Leaving his clothes in a pile on the grass he walked into the water and was not seen alive again. Lines from Australian poems I once had to memorise circle my head as I hold my nephew's hands in my own to lift him over the waves. *What does he do with them all, the old king:/Having such a shining haul of boys in his sure net,/How does he keep them happy, lead them to forget/The world above, the aching air, birds, spring?* The lines remind me of English lessons in hot weatherboard portables after the holidays are over, the agony of having to recite in front of the teacher, but the pleasure, anyway, in the seduction of the language, in the melancholy or exhilarated state that a piece of writing can bestow. English lessons made me hopeful enough to fend off the terrible loneliness of the school years and were a kind of permission to plunge into my own early attempts at writing. I find these early poems and passages in old diaries or on scraps of paper acting as bookmarks in abandoned textbooks. I read of the secret love I hold for my schoolteacher and of other sad things.

It is impossible that I ever wrote these melodramas, I think, sorting through old suitcases of schoolwork, knowing they cannot fit in the writing-room shed I will one day build, let alone in the caravan where I've been writing for the past four years. How could so many years have gone by anyway that the nieces and the nephews agonise over which aunt–mother is which from photographs of that time? They try to be tactful, but really my sisters and I can see they are making little more than wild stabs in the dark. That they cannot see the child we once were in our faces of today, even with the photograph of the child right before them, is a sobering thought.

Whenever the children come to visit I take photos. I have albums full now, with the exact same backdrop of my A-shaped tarpaulin draped over the ridgepole, the river, the framing leaves of the lantana and whalebone tree. The children swarm into my caravan, eager to see the latest albums and the old ones they know I've been searching through.

These old holiday photographs are the kind new lovers are always shown. Somehow it is more vital than almost anything else, in those first early weeks, to give the new person some glimmer of how full of life you once were. Here, you are saying, without using words, this was my special self, this was me, less tarnished, less worried, more hopeful, infinitely observant. See, how uncovered by fat my bones once were? Family albums are pilfered. You want to turn back into the photograph child you proffer to your new lover, hoping that in this way evidence of old relationship wounds and the wrinkles coursing like some kind of land erosion across parts of your face will be miraculously waived. You want the new lover to see the beautiful lines in your lips before those very lines began to cross into the skin under your nose and mouth.

I warm immediately to people with strong childhood memories. On the other hand if people tell me they can remember nothing of their childhood or its holidays I look at them carefully, wondering what reason have they to lie. I love to meet women and men who can recollect crying their eyes out on the car journey home from holidays.

One of my favourite things when I am small, is to press out pictures and photographs using pins, not scissors. I sit with my still straight back at school, painstakingly moving a pin around the edges of a piece of fruit or a yellow dog. The more impatient pupils rip their pictures or abandon them altogether, but I can never get enough of this kind of job. My writing reminds me of these old activities and hopes, for it seems clear to me that not only am I still living on my father's farm but that I'm quite unable to stop trying to press out the shapes of the past. No memory, no matter how small or insignificant, must be torn, and my pen is the pin I use. I always write with the finest nib available. A drawing pen is best. On summer days the ink flows so unevenly that when I shake it in frustration black shapes splatter into the writing. Sometimes I see an animal's face has landed in the pattern of the ink, or that if I move the pen from words into pictures I can draw a girl in a dress holding a furred beast in her hands as she looks up into the sky. It is when staring into the strange faces and animals that grow next to paragraphs and sentences that the most forgotten memories sometimes arrive; that I'll remember a piece of writing which instantly illuminates the very memory I have been labouring to locate with my small black words.

On bad days the harder I try to pinpoint the past, the more it recedes, and then I am reminded of the slides that have fared the worst over time: though I try to remove the film with the utmost care from its old Kodak mount, like an ancient beetle it is ready to fall apart in my hands. There is the opposite sensation too that, although past incidents can be disassembled and broken off into their component parts, they have the capacity to be surculose, to spring back into new life in the way of a broken off piece of starfish.

One day I'm going to build myself a writing shed using straw-bales and old doors, with a particularly steep roof the main architectural point. Meanwhile, there is the faded blue aluminium writing van, manufactured the year I was born, which lately has also become the meditation van. I used to hate caravans, displaying the family preference for voluminous canvas tents, but this one has endeared itself to me like an old fat dog. I like the way the cows seem to find it a comforting presence too, gathering with their calves on Sundays to hear the listener requests on the classical FM station. However could I have eaten osso bucco, I wonder, looking at the perfection of a pair of black calf ears, or the way their white lashes drape low over their eyes. The van is thirteen by seven feet and though I have to duck at either end on account of its curved ceilings there is never a feeling of claustrophobia, due to every large and little window looking out towards water. I bought the van from a Buddhist family far from the coast. Some previous owner must have towed it to the sea every now and then because each time a linoleum tile lifts up, there is a scattering of white sand, and in the cupboard above the left wheel, a cartwheel shell.

Sometimes I wonder who might have the van after me and what a puzzle it will be to them, trying to work out the meanings of the sentences and chapter beginnings I like to scribble straight onto the walls. Yvonne says that the van will never have another owner because the day will soon come when my van's going to suddenly collapse in on itself in the way of an old pumpkin. Next to a line of Basho haikus I keep pinned by a curtain, she scribbles her own:

> CARAVAN AT AUTUMN'S END,
> LIKE FADED BLUE PUMPKIN
> SO QUIET AND STILL.

The shape of the past, I think, is like that of the hungry mosquito hanging in the near darkness by the thin gauze door: the closer I believe I am to reaching its outline, the more uncertain I become of its position.

II   BEATAE MEMORIAE [L.]   *Of Blessed Memories*

The beach of memories is always Diggers Camp, where my family and I have been coming for over a quarter of a century. There were other childhood beaches, Noosa when it was still small and quiet, Broken Head or Sandon Rivers, but I can't remember the shape of their headlands or alongside which trees the tent was pitched or the families who accompanied us.

At Diggers Camp there is still no zebra crossing full of icecream eaters. To return to the site where the family tent used to be pitched, where campers are no longer allowed, is to find myself searching for the ghosts of the children we were. From this spot you can see the sun rising, and sometimes in winter the passage of whales heading north, their spouts echoing your own leap of faith as you move along the headland, keeping them in sight. There is no shop, no electricity, and tin tanks have always stood beside or behind every shack and cottage like some household temple to the rainwater gods. During January the heath fills with Christmas bells too elegant and sculptural, too euphorically coloured, to be real. There are grass trees too, like incense sticks waiting for a large match.

One day, heartbroken at the ending of a long-distance love affair, I drive out to Diggers at 4 a.m. and steal a Christmas bell. It stays on my desk like a yellow and crimson miracle, causing me equal levels of joy and guilt as I tap its top, making it move in a tall glass of water and formulating reasons to my ex-lover as to why we are making a terrible mistake. When there is no reply to my letter I retreat to Diggers Camp for a week. I barely see another soul for all of the seven days, walking melodramatically through the mauve sea sand, my feet rising and falling through the foam of old mermaids, rising and falling, rising and falling, until I have walked all day, nearly reaching the beach of Angourie before I have found any peace with my new solitary state.

If only all the anxiety and stress of an adult life could be chopped down like a big clump of mistletoe from around my neck, then I feel I would be young again and agile, the waves curling in endlessly from the swells beyond North Solitary Island, everyone alive still under the black cockatoos – the yellow-tailed *Calyptorhynchus funereus* that come wheeling in from the heathlands – and not just connected up to slanting memories of who they might have been before I was old enough to ask. One of the camping boys who had skin even more olive than our own died on a motorbike when he was a young man, but I will always remember him as the boy he once was. He was the best body-surfer, his teeth as white as the tops of waves or the cream on top of the homemade scone he once proffered me, cream from his cow with only the faintest dusting of crunchy sand.

At Diggers Camp you can be any age you want to be. You can be seventeen with your schoolteacher on a towel in the hot grass, or twenty-nine and falling in love with a woman on the beach where important things have always happened, where your five-year-old self is quite close to who you are today. Looking into the woman's eyes reminds you of the way the colour changes suddenly between the shallows and the deep ocean slicing over the continental shelf. At Diggers Camp you can be an eternal aunt years on from now, feeling your way barefoot along the shore on old feet the colour of the pippies that slip through the sand and tides. Then the lines of sand from the tide marks will be like some kind of seam, not only echoing the pattern of wrinkles mysteriously engrained across your forehead but helping somehow to join up all the stories.

Writing is one way of putting a life into perspective, but like an aunt from the olden days I piece together many other things: photos into albums, posies into vases, squares of knitting into rugs with the names of the children at one end and their dogs at the other, leaves into compost, lines of poetry into sand using purple coral sticks and the best part of the afternoon. The suspicion has begun to grow stronger in me that there will never be an end to all this assembling and that when I die much will still be left. My notebooks, I think, my wool bags, will never be emptied or filled, and what will anybody ever make of all these bits and pieces, these stories abandoned or so half told it is impossible to know the ending? Who sees the writing I leave in the sand at Diggers by poets or writers so long dead even their names have gone missing? Does anyone else read the Basho about bells and flowers before the wind or the water brushes the fine coral sideways? Does it matter if the answer is no one?

If the state of enlightenment must ultimately be present in even the most simple and everyday of acts, how can one ever reconcile this to writing, which has always been for me such an energetic swerving between past and present? Then I think that in wool or in watercolours anyway I might have a better chance of catching the holiday world of the childhood beach, or of the early Field Naturalists Club camps – or that possibly something even more ephemeral, coloured sands, would be most suitable of all. Some kind of bright mandala to be blown away, to vanish as childhood itself does.

THE FIRST STORIES IN MY childhood are told in front of the campfire or, once we are all bedded down, by the glow of the hurricane lantern. Our father makes up stories about Simba and Serina, two lions, or the animals who live under Humpty Doo Bridge. As he recites a bit of Gunga Din I imagine how the sea is carrying a tidal wave our way that will sweep us and the tent into the sea. Then it will be our mother's seahorse, larger of course than the small dead ones occasionally found on the beach, who will save us from certain destruction. It will be a hippocampus and we will be four children in a line on the magical half-horse, half-mermaid back.

When the stories are over and our father tells us how this part of the day, this sleeping part, is the best, I make noises of disbelief. I'm not tired at all. I'll never sleep, I think, listening to the waves arriving and leaving the beach and watching the shadows of my mother and father, huge now against the canvas walls, as they too come down into their sleeping-bags; my mother not my father always the one to lift the lantern's glass, to turn down the wick and blow out the light with the same kind of sound as when she sends us an aerial kiss.

In the mornings on the beach I canter up to where my mother lies with her head on a makeshift pillow of sand. She is on her side reading a book and I cannot see her eyes through the greenness of her sunglasses. In fact her whole face is nearly hidden under the brim of the huge navy-blue Panama hat that is worn for all of these holidays of my early childhood.

I run underneath the waterspout, the old goldmining pipe that jets fresh water from the wetlands onto the beach, and back to my mother. I roll into my sand castle, at this age so unseparated from the elements that to be wet and sandy is not a horrible sensation. My mother gives me a fruit bonbon from her handbag before returning to her book. The pineapple sweetness is part of the wonderful morning, watching the sea, my sisters and the Sneath children doing handstands in the waves.

My names are Nipsy, Nipsy Beetle, Nipsle, Gilly or Gillybags but I am also a child aunt or an eternal aunt in her childhood years, watching her family in its endless configurations and patterns as it moves across the beach we have always called ours, and which the nine nieces and nephews also think of as theirs – but only the southern section, with one pandanus in particular. So that to walk into its shade feels as right as walking into one of our houses.

A child aunt likes to hover near her mother's ankles, and apart from certain essential activities in the sea generally prefers the company of mothers to fathers. Auntish qualities are already laid down in her character, long before she is really an actual aunt.

One day, a child aunt, grown up in a shorter amount of time than seems possible and possibly having no children of her own, will devote numerous days, months, perhaps even years of her life lavishing a particular kind of love onto the children of her sisters or friends. At moments, these children will so resemble herself or her sisters or her own mother and father in the very old photo albums that the aunt will feel a creeping sadness, a sense of disaster underneath skin that no longer resembles a milky-white nut. Wings, unhinging like messages from insects in her water buckets, can fill her with an emptiness so sudden she might pull off her shirt to imagine the baby that has never been born. She watches the strong tongues of calves and tries not to stare at breastfeeding mothers at the markets on Sundays.

Sometimes, there will be family get-togethers that include people who were with us at the Naturalists Club camps of childhood. Although we might not have seen one another for years, the old connections stay fine and strong like the best kind of guy rope. Even if we didn't always go to each other's weddings we imagine we did, and giant gatherings continue to occur in kitchens, or some of the most memorable camps are alluded to wistfully in intermittent correspondences.

Eileen Sneath's laugh summons the presence of camping mothers who can't be present – Marie Morris, Margaret Mylrea, Mrs Moreton and my own mother, known to other children as Mrs Mears – the real heroes of any of the camping trips. They had the mammoth task of preparing the food, clothes and first-aid kits containing enough bandaids for their children and everyone else's as well, at the same time maintaining their patience and the possibility of glee.

'My goodness,' says our father coming into the kitchen where the main core reminiscing is taking place. 'I know that for Eric and Peter and me, camping was great fun. You know! We'd go and come home and be back at work on Monday, but poor Sheila and Eileen and Margaret! They'd be wading through washing for a week, getting maggots out of wet clothes and trying to find out where all the cutlery could've gone.'

The pickings in the kitchen where we're all sitting are scarce enough to resemble the final hours of a camping expedition. Due to lack of space the Sneaths are even being accommodated in one of the old twelve- by twelve-foot canvas tents that we've never owned and still hire. Someone has been married but this seems less important than the cracking pace of reminiscence. The motley array of food includes green potatoes, a bit of old wine and cheese, fresh bread, chocolate, tea, coffee, fruit and peanuts from which our father is dusting the salt. Children are whizzing about the grown-ups with an exhausted bright glaze over their eyes and homemade Fanta icypoles in their hands.

'This is just like old times,' people keep saying as posses of children roam about with combs and gel doing the hair of grown-ups in strange shapes, using ribbons and spray. The two girls who are most like Able Seaman Susan in the *Swallows and Amazons* books are torn between abandoning themselves to the chaos and trying to find their lost sandals. They are the two with the greatest affinity for wool and for words and who at the Lionsville camp last winter could be seen wading into the middle of the creek to fetch the best running water, even though it meant freezing their feet blue.

The hairdressing scene is possibly wilder than the 1960s – more liberties with parents, a later night – but I can feel the past is floating close by us, filling us all with that particular shade of laughter that is close to

sorrow. And there goes another child aunt. Even though he is a small boy, I call him child aunt in secret due to all his familiar tendencies. It is his affinity with insects and gardens, his way of watching events from the sidelines, and just now how he came quietly past wearing an old alpaca poncho, a packet of marshmallows in his hand. When I poke my head around his bedroom door, he is snipping open the packet using the pair of miniature scissors on his birthday penknife, and as well as having a candle over which to toast them knows roughly how many each child might expect to eat once they are divided into columns. He is called B for short, and soon after I have seen him being born a butterfly comes into the garden each day for a week to land on his head. It's clear from the blue-winged butterfly's behaviour that no flower can smell quite as sweet and powdery as the softest part of his skull, pulsing in the sun with new life.

'My name is Treat today,' he tells me. Or, 'Hello,' he says. 'I'm Shaky Town.' Or, 'My name is Nothing.' He is the child, sitting with just his pair of elephant socks on, who sees with sudden recognition the similarities between the eggs the sugar ants are carrying into a crack in the wall and the ricebubbles floating in the milk in his bowl.

Like a memory of myself, the child aunts like to make the family breakfast. At the small cooking fire under the whalebone tree, they crouch down low to blow on the coals. They make a big billy full of porridge, running over to the van for milk and yoghurt and adding particular ingredients in consultation with each other or with me – dried fruit or shredded coconut – with serious aplomb and a barely concealed irritation if someone tries to talk before all the bowls are filled.

Whenever people ask me how it is possible that I could've lived outside for so long, I want to reply, However could anyone remove themselves so completely from the sensations of childhood camping? I write to them about the blessing of bare feet again. I mention meditating one day on the river rock for so long that the tide rose up above my ankles and began to fall again, the water like some kind of skin unpeeling. But unless they have at least some camping history it's nearly futile to mention that I haven't been this happy for years. I try to tell them about the child aunts but when words fall short, when my sentences begin to die, I take out my camera instead.

I take a photograph of the three child aunts, and the sun catching in the gold light around their heads makes them seem to be a part of some sacred, not family, picture.

A CORRESPONDENT WHOSE LETTERS I possibly cherish above all others once gave me the advice that only by sifting through photographs and listening to the memories that arrive in faces just glimpsed in the shadow of old-fashioned cars or campfire smoke will I ever come into my true writing. Gillian, he wrote, if you do not find the time to do this, I fear you will eventually write the kind of work that I will no longer be able to read.

I write back to say that if only he could see the tiny caravan where I write, waiting for the day when the eternal aunt's shed is not just a dream, then he would understand that I have been following his advice for years. The pale, auntish-blue walls are pinned with photographs so frail now from sunlight that they make me think of a butterfly collection. One day they will disintegrate altogther but I cannot bear not to have the old images about me, my attachment to them growing stronger even as the photographic paints crack like enamel, or grow new meanings with the mildews of this wet summer marching across on little green legs.

Long before I'm a writer I'm already engrossed in the business of old photographs. At the age of thirteen when my father begins divvying up the family silver, I say I'd far prefer photographs to any jug or teaspoon. Couldn't I be the caretaker of all the family albums? I ask, and receive them into my custodianship without the ceremony with which I believe they are due. Particularly on wet days I like to take out the oldest album of all where women in long white dresses in Africa or India sit on little seats next to a car on a beach, waiting for their water to boil for a cup of tea. I like to peer into their long faces trying to ascertain what their personalities may have been, whether they would have laughed softly or with riotous disregard for the men standing in a group nearby. I wish that the owner of the albums had thought to label the photographs for the benefit of the future, that she had put the address of the house where the empty cane chair rocks on the edge of the verandah.

The permission to look to your heart's content at a photo reminds me of walking away from the group of family and friends under the pandanus palm, down to the waves. During this walk you can be sure that whatever your age everyone will be watching you, analysing the shape of your bottom, your bogspavined knees or turned-in ankles, the sudden hairiness of your thighs now you're in your thirties or the miraculous lack thereof if you're still a child.

In the garden, in the hill paddock where the writing shed will one day be built, there are already flowering bushes and flowers and two old foambark trees. One of the foambarks has a branch like a ladder curved up from the ground and B and the child aunts like to climb into the tree with me, there to look down on the family.

For once, with the word aunt, dictionaries fail me. Where are the subtle emanations of love, kindness and duty in their bald descriptions? The common childless aunt holds a quality of love more intense in some ways than mother love, in that it cannot help but be underlined by the sense of loss – of not having had a child. I call the laughter that passes between my surrogate children and me storm laughter, in that it intoxicates the air in a similar way, affecting us like wild negative ions.

A dictionary of Aboriginal words offers a rich list of aunt words. *Apu, biwi, mama, maman yok, nerbet, piny, pipi, yayu*, I read. This is more like it. I think with sharp sorrow of my one and only aunt, on the other side of Australia, who no longer writes to me because she is afraid some part of one letter or another will end up in a story. Pledges and promises make no difference. Fear has lost me her friendship. Clearly she thinks, after that last book or story, that I am not to be trusted. Her photo face is on my wall too, her elegant eyes turned away from mine as she sits in front of her huge loom. Even though she no longer writes I think she might understand why I call the koel the aunt bird, its call as sonorous yet sad as the word aunt itself – and heralding changes, marking always for me the passing of old patterns and seasons.

Working in wool, I think ruefully, is far less hazardous. I cannot imagine any hand-loomed rug or jumper from my aunt's hands has ever caused anything but pleasure. If only writing could be so pure. If only I could say that my words had always caused happiness.

I'd like a writing room with a roof like a hat, I've always said, but what I've really meant, I realise, is a room like a tent in the shape of the old camping tents from childhood, only wood not canvas walls, but that same air of both comfort and festivity that comes immediately with a roof with a steep enough pitch. The tent under which I've lived these last few years has a tear in it near my pillow that lets in starlight and a clearer sound of the pre-dawn mopoke. To enter the space of a tent is to enter the bare minimum of clutter, with the most complicated shape belonging to the hurricane lantern.

For your eyes to alight on my room on a rainy day amongst the trees will give the same feeling of pleasure as coming in from a long circular bushwalk in 1968 or 1969 would have bought, to see the family tent from a different angle, the smell of frying onions meaning some wonderful mother had defeated the drizzling odds to make a strong cooking fire.

The writing room's windows will arrest the gaze in the same way as the most fabulous of insects that the child aunts show me. 'Once,' I tell them, 'I used to hide in one of Sonya's grass traps, pretending I was the kind of spider that only liked to go out in secret.' B turns to feed the baby a sardine on toast. 'Did you?' he asks carefully. 'Had you a lid you could pull shut?' I say that, yes, there was a lid, imagining it clearly as I speak, of woven grass into which I could crawl whenever I needed to be alone, or into which I would take some insect or another for closer observation – as if in doing so when I was a child, at the end of the holidays, the bigger sadness might have been inexplicably lessened. The bigger sadness was to do with the iodine bushes at the farm lit with hard yellow fruit, the breasts of sisters, tears falling on my blue flannelette sheet at night, new friends and the feeling of days passing that could never come back.

'I lined the inside of my secret place with purple silk,' I say, elaborating on my story which is half-fabrication, half-truth, with an image from the Laurens van der Post novel I'm reading and memories of the trapdoors on the paths at Binna Burra. Upon hearing this final detail the child aunts look at me with such wholesale admiration that I cannot say it is only a story really, that Sonya's camouflaged holes were for tripping you up in, not refuge, and that it is only long since that I have imagined the safety of such a place to a growing child – the warm grass, the light peeping in through the lid, a cubby more complete than any ever built. Too late to confess as the children ask could I help make three in the back paddock, only if possible could the silk be blue and not purple?

'*Se non è vero, è ben trovato,*' I mutter to myself, hoping Sonya hasn't been listening. If it's not true, it's well invented. I walk with the children to their present cluster of cubby-houses. They stand like a shanty town behind a patch of rainforest, made of dead palm fronds, cardboard boxes, ripped horse rugs and ropes.

'I don't want this, Aunt Onion,' says a child aunt who still has trouble with my name, handing me back the teacup of orange cordial. 'It's too glassable.'

The light behind the foambark changes. I see it deepening in exquisite runs along the trunk and more than ever the fruit has the appearance of the kind of scarlet velvet a child of six would so much suit for a winter dress. I rush to undo my camera case. The haste is so I don't lose forever the way afternoon light is landing on a child's face and the hollows of her limbs. It is the kind of light that years later will illuminate things beyond the mere shape of her face or the fuzzy quality around the ponytail dried into a stiff point.

'Oh,' says Sonya, whose camera went out of action years ago as her life became too busy, 'it's so nice to have a documentary aunt in the family.' One Christmas at the farm, I listened to a sister saying how that other sister's baby's head didn't smell as nice as her baby's, and the soothing of pride, the reassurances I must offer to the annoyed mother who has overheard the comment, is all part of being an aunt. So is being punished for your childlessness. A sister snaps at me about not understanding about the children. She adds that when she and our other sisters are not being bad mothers, they are very good mothers.

For a moment I must turn away so she can't see the extent of the wound. I gather up a child who is quite stricken and sad himself due to the fact that his superman cape has not taken him jetting up into the air. I want to laugh and cry, reminded of my own bitter disappointment when the Glasshouse Mountains turned out to be not fragile and not see-through, and the Coloured Sands anything but magical in their dun-coloured hue under the persistent rain of that Queensland holiday.

III   ANNUS MIRABILIS [L.]   *Year of Wonder*

Although the beetle name gradually fades from favour, the intonation of the water birds on the lagoon near the dunes at Diggers Camp makes me see that these are the best years of all. These are the religious years too, when I will ask my mother for a bible for Christmas and squint seriously at the tiny print, unable to know that in less than six years' time I will scribble at the front of this very same bible the crap word and others worse still, and annoy my father, refusing to say in church the bit about not being good enough to gather up the crumbs from under the table. But at the age of seven or eight I like to see the nuns in the convent next door to school, enjoying their calm faces under their habits. I look with all due care at the watercolour of Jesus standing on flowering grasses. I don't actually need to read the Book of Matthew in order to consider the lilies of the field or the birds of the air, for I have not reached the awful age of adolescence when I stop doing so. On a walk along the heath I stare into the trumpeting colour of a Christmas bell with such longing it takes all the urging of my mother to leave it growing so other people also can enjoy its late flowering.

On the beach the sand breaks up between my toes in a way that makes me think of a tray of biscuits, and the night crabs have laid the lower beach with sandballs so cool I lie down in them. Here is a shell that looks as if it has been fried in gold and pink light. And isn't this one just like a raspberry flummery? A few years ago I would have put it in my mouth but already I'm older. The grease from a grown-up's nose is useful to shine up shells and sea-stones, if you can persuade them of the worthiness of the cause. I'm going to be tall, everyone keeps promising, and already in the family photographs my extra inches make me seem the eldest.

I sit on my mother's legs, still small enough for this to be possible, as she pours fresh water over my hair and lathers in a drop of shampoo. The water spout gushes behind us, the sea is ahead. English beaches were all stones, she says, her feet inside the little stone dam we built yesterday to change the flow of water down to the sea. I hear her telling me about the German and Chinese goldminers who once brought their diggings to this very spout to be rinsed, and that once, before this, the beach was known as Fairy Bower.

Only many years after we have first camped at Diggers as a family do I find out that it was once a special beach to the Gumbayngirr tribe. Near the old midden it's easy to imagine the women and children walking in from the river country in times of trouble or sickness, but when I'm seven or eight no one tells me that history. I don't know their stories, I don't know that it was a beach for women and children, and if I stand next to my naked mother, seeing how like little spiderwebs is the water from her wash, caught in the black hair in her lap, nothing in me knows that a long time ago an Aboriginal child may have had just such a thought about her own mother or auntie.

The sea is very safe, protected from the southerly swells by a large rock-shelf where the best shells are found. Having the spout pleases the grown-ups who can wash the salt from themselves after swimming, and reminds me of the cascades seen in the forests at Binna Burra, my family's other special holiday place on the Lamington Plateau where we go whenever our mother is lacking camping stamina. The water is nearly as cool. I like to open my mouth up underneath it to feel the weight of the water pulling my cheeks down and sideways.

Every now and then I look up into my mother's talking, laughing face. I see the marine light going into her mouth and coming out in her smile, through the gap in her front teeth. Without makeup her eyes are smaller, friendlier. Diggers Camp has always acted like a charm on our mother, peeling something back in her so that we see another, funnier, happier, layer. Her handbag with its array of cosmetics has been left behind and later, when the day's warmer, she'll spit watermelon seeds through the gap in her teeth in a way she never would at home. Her low-hanging breasts are soft to the touch. I am very much aware of them even if I have long ago forgotten the taste of their milk.

Light spins through branches into the creek where I sit with my mother, landing in the shape of the eye I have already seen in other places. I have seen it in the Binna Burra forests in its most immense form, slanting through the beech trees, a huge light-filled iris illuminating the forest floor before dark. Or, equally large, in the biblical sunsets, shooting through rainclouds. The eye shrinks into a cup of tea for my father, settling out as I add evaporated milk, and the same sort of eye looks up into my own from the bottom of the silver thermos. Secretly I long to believe it could be the eye of God, but when I confide this to a sister she says witheringly that she hasn't read an account yet to say that God is a Cyclops and that what, anyway, would his eye be doing lying in the middle of a circle of sliced carrot, or in the potato cut in half that I hold up for her to see.

Although this sarcasm is daunting, whenever I say my curious prayer at night – a kind of line of names and hopes – I open one of my own eyes, seeing if in the dark there is any light-filled eye shining into mine.

Only occasionally do I fret about some kind of answer or sign of reply. I turn a torch on in the hood of my sleeping-bag and there is an eye there too, glassy and yellow, with a dark pupil. I pray to the torchlight that I will see a shark tomorrow, and that though it will eat neither me nor anyone else it will glide in through the breakers, close enough for us all to see the shape of a grey killer's eye. I keep my eyes pressed shut, asking for the most beautiful cowrie to be delivered into my keeping on the shell walks with my mother that lie ahead. I pray for the lagoon to be at low tide so that I can take my mother, who cannot swim, over to the endless rocks and shells of the southern end.

By 1997 a move is afoot to stop the taking of shells, either dead or alive, from the Diggers Camp beach and rock-shelves. Ecologically sound though this is, I cannot help but feel the sadness of such a rule being hung in place next to the signs about no dogs, no horses, no fires and no gathering of firewood. The proposal sends me rummaging around to locate my old cowrie collection. There are hundreds of them, their surfaces flecked with colours found in human eyes or washed to the blind blue of the man who used to sit on the edge of his Diggers shack verandah, drinking tea so black my father said it should come with stars. According to the environmental rules of the nineties, it's clear that I have deprived the beach of a considerable amount of calcium but I would no more dream of returning any shells than I would my potsherds from ancient Greek sites, or the Roman coin found near Hadrian's Wall with my father.

The thought of a child having to break a rule in order to add to her shell collection weighs in me. I remember how I used to pack cowries in my sewing case, tucking them into samplers and failed pin cushions. A shell could be a small oval of comfort in your hand as the sewing teacher lost her temper, and a hidden pleasure lay in their lips that you could kiss without anyone realising what you were doing.

At Diggers Camp when I'm eight or nine, my mother and I seek not only cowrie shells but dead crabs or their claws, the mechanics of the nippers more marvellous almost than the crimson vein along the side, the spray of colour and pattern something a watercolour illustrator could ask to replicate only in her most hopeful dreams. As we round the headland onto the long beach that leads north, we come upon Sonya, Karin and Yvonne fishing, our father on patient standby to fix up lines and hooks lost to seaweed or rocks, and to cast out Sonya's yellow handline, because each time she feels the tug of a wave she's convinced she has a fish. She is so excited the morning that a fish really does take her bait that instead of winding in the line, she bounds towards us and the headland and trees. Away from the seawater her sunfish glitters and gleams. It is like pieces of my best mother-of-pearl shell glued onto a living fish. Other children, Sneath boys and Sneath girls, are also forgetting to wind in their handlines, just running and hauling as the bream that I can see swimming in each green wave begin to bite. The wet sand is a mirror to all the running legs, which are so brown it's impossible they ever were much paler, with red lines from school socks and garters.

To eat fragments of these fish from the frying pans Mrs Sneath has going on the fire is like eating buttered early-morning light, the filaments of life falling apart under my tongue. Only the boy catching toadfish in the lagoon misses out, but when he shows me one of his dead toadies I can sort of understand his preference for fish so poisonous and ugly. He is the quiet boy with the preference for picking up other people's fishing rubbish from the muddy sand among the mangroves.

Isn't this also the day that I find the largest cowrie I ever will, or have I somehow condensed every wonderful thing into one day, one holiday?

The shell's flawed, as if something went wrong with the creature who once lived within. The dappled, deerlike sides remind me of Marjorie Rawlings' *The Yearling*, or of old brood mares in spring. God has his eye on me I know as I pick it up from its place in the sand underneath the rockpool ledge. It rattles with what sounds like a coin, but as I shake it a silver pendant emerges. A lady is pictured with her arms outstretched, flowers circling her head. My mother emits an irritated sigh and says that Catholicism is everywhere, even on an empty Australian beach. A Child of Mary medallion, my mother says, such as she herself once had to wear, with a blue cloak and white veil.

'*Sancta Maria, sine labe originali concepta, ora pro nobisi,*' reads my mother. On the other side a cross threads through the letter M. More stars and then what look to be two ripe strawberries complete the picture. It is my first taste of Latin and I am enchanted. They are not strawberries, my mother explains, but the sacred heart of Jesus and his mother, bleeding and lying open to remind us of suffering. Then my mother's voice changes as if, after all, it's only a load of hogwash.

THE RAIN SETS IN HEAVILY in the night and I am not sure which is the most thrilling, the sound of it on canvas or the wilder sea I can hear growing closer with every wave. In the middle of the night our father lights the hurricane lantern. He has flung a woollen blanket over his shoulders and it crackles with static electricity. Over the sea it looks as if someone is turning a large fluorescent light on and off, on and off. Our father herds us into the middle of the tent, away from the walls which are running with water in the way I imagine sails must do, or duck wings.

From a raft of dry bedding in the morning, we watch our mother cook up an extraordinary breakfast of bacon, egg and bean rolls, using only the small green primus at the front of the tent and donations of food from the other families, who've decided to pack up fast in case the roads home flood. We peep out every now and then at the wet mothers and fathers and at the vague outlines of children captured in steamed-up stagion wagons where they've been ordered to stay dry.

Later, as the rain contines without remorse and everyone else has left, our mood only seems to heighten. Our father checkmates our mother on the travelling chess set and we play the card games cheat, fish, murder and strip-Jack-naked. When I lick the tent wall there is less salt, more mould and I see the patterns forming are like patterns of lichen on old rock. Up near the centre pole the rain has brought on the premature birth of hundreds of baby daddy-long-legs, lighter looking than any feeling I know as they spill into their mother's web.

After lunch the rain lessens enough for us to go onto the beach in our swimmers. The rock-shelf is mainly hidden by sea, except for some long pieces like beached whales by the shore. I would like to discover something exciting, a dead body of some kind, but the sea has swept the first beach clean of even its normal pebbles.

When I come dashing around the corner to see the rockpool where I found the cowrie and the icon I have to stop to take stock, for the rocks look as if someone has come in the rain and iced them pink. I lean in closer, over the rockpool with its waving weeds, bottle-green sea velvet, and barnacles like craters on the moon. The rocks have always been slightly pink but it is the afternoon light making every colour more intense. It is Him, I think, looking to see if I can catch an eye anywhere in sight. Even if there is not a shark for me, there is a shark-egg case, gnarled and tough in my mother's hand, and sponges she calls dead man's fingers.

Not until evening when we are once again about to go to sleep do I clearly feel that he's somewhere above the roof of the tent. I can hear wings in the tree under which we are camped and as the small volleys of wind hit the canvas every now and then, nothing would surprise me less than if the wings turn out to be attached to our tent. Flying thus like a giant canvas butterfly I'll have full view of him at last, all his eyes looking into my family's own small brown ones and my mother's sea-grey ones with the same type of look, the same kindness of Mr and Mrs Mylrea, Mr and Mrs Morris or Mr and Mrs Sneath, who unfortunately have left the headland early and won't be here for this meeting with the God of my eight-year-old self. Perhaps, I go to sleep thinking, he will have rows of eyes like hunting spiders have, but large and soulful and alive with the light of happy omens.

IV   IN MEDIAS RES [L.]   *Into the Midst of Things*

The two main pleasures of preparing to leave the house for a tent are food and books. We go with our mother to the librarian, who allows us to borrow eight books each for the holiday ahead, and then with our father to the bookshop for one new book each. The books we borrow or buy are fairy tales of the world, Tove Jansson, Arthur Ransome, Nan Chauncy, Ivan Southall, Colin Thiele, Hugh Lofting, Susan Cooper, Alan Garner, Hobberdy Dick, Mary O'Hara, Rosemary Harris, Patricia Wrightson, and although we solemnly promise not to read the library books on the beach, it's with great shame at the end of each holiday that we drop the books through the after-hours slot, their plastic dust-covers rattling with sand.

When I cast an eye into the boxes of food waiting in the middle of the sitting room I am not disappointed by my mother's efforts. There are real and tinned puddings, a crate for bread alone, boxes of fruit, vegetables, a spare Christmas cake, packets of shop biscuits, homemade shortbreads with edible green baubles, beans, dried apricots, tinned apricots, and real ones from Mr Permise's. For lunch along the way in a basket with packets of chips, are chicken wings all whiskery and cold wrapped in a tea towel.

She has thought so much of everything that I don't mind her asking me to check for any tomatoes left in the garden. I find the bushes all but dead, as if they know there's no use growing anymore now that the family is going away. The few left are beyond eating and more than any other thing resemble the old yellow dog's testicles from up the road.

I wish there had been time to give the ducks a last swim. We're in the habit of marching with a duck under each arm, down the steep hill to Mr Greenwood the farmer's cattle trough. After their swim the ducks take lumbering flight, very white against the blue sky and beating us back to the house. But there is no time for that, says Yvonne, latching shut the duck pen. No time to wade around in the trough with our swimmers on, feeling the slime between our toes and watching the water boatmen.

Even as we are limiting the joy of the ducks, our own suddenly seems more certain. The stricken face of our dog pressed against the station wagon's glass as he is driven away to the kennels before the car is loaded brings the same mix of feelings. We are going to Lamington Plateau or Mt Barney, Diggers Camp or Hanging Rock Station near the Mann. Who knows now exactly where we are heading in 1974 or 1975 or whatever year it is as Sonya and I, still little enough to be climbing head first into the back of the car, watch our father winding up the back window. So much sugar from Christmas icing boils around in our bodies that it is almost certain there will be a yell from one of us in an hour or so, or whenever the first stretch of winding road is reached, to *Stop the car!*, before we are sick all over the sisters sitting below us.

On the way, lolling high up on the mattresses with Sonya drawing faces on my toes with a red texta pen, I begin to learn the first Latin I've encountered since the words on the Child of Mary medallion. *Beatae memoriae,* I say, with no idea at all of pronunciation. *Annus mirabilis*, year of wonder, I find at the back of my *Collins English Gem Dictionary*. Latin is not taught anymore in country high schools, where I will be going next year, so I must seek it where I may.

'*In medias res*,' I say aloud. Into the midst of things. The car is taking us through the avenues of trees whose majestic roots remind us of the forests ahead. The domestic smells of towns – mown grass, cement footpaths, machinery, roses, the bakery – will soon disappear. At Mt Barney or Diggers Camp we'll eat all of our food from a bowl and our breakfast cereal in enamel mugs. The porridge will taste of burnt billy but we'll be so hungry the charcoal will only add substance.

Our father is driving with one arm out the window and every now and then he turns to say something to our mother. In our perched position Sonya and I have totally blocked our father's rear-vision mirror, but we can see everything. Our parents' profiles are interesting to watch, or we can peer down into the crooked white partings of Karin and Yvonne's hair, checking for dandruff and moles. We are going on holidays and nothing can dim our mood, not even the sight of the girl at the last house of town jumping up and down by herself with a trickling hose on her trampoline. Somewhere along the way roadworkers will be passed. Though our mother tells us sorrowfully that using the jackhammers will turn their hands to jelly by the time they are forty, the sight of them so hot by the side of yellow machinery somehow adds to being a child on a mattress with a dictionary, three mint leaves left in a little white packet, two orange squashes and the whole of the holidays ahead.

We've been coming to the same holiday places for so long I know the exact moment when the first glimpse of sea will meet our eyes, or around which corner the first bellbird will send its clear notes through the open window. The air will become saltier or cooler.

Our parents are still under the age of forty. They may be the age I am now as I write this and from afar I admire their resolution, their patience and their energy as they head with their family into the hills or coastal heathlands.

Once off the bitumen, our father takes off his seatbelt and we are allowed to ride in towards the other Naturalists Club campers on top of the tent on the rusty roof-racks. We smack the hot roof with open hands in the hope that our father might be persuaded to go faster. Or we hang down over the windscreen pulling faces to make our mother shake her head, smiling, but with something already tired in anticipation of the days ahead around the lines near her mouth. Still, her gold filling glints with good humour as she leans out of the window to raise an arm in greeting to Margaret Mylrea or Marie Morris.

Looking back, I think of the mothers as being like beleaguered sergeant majors before the fray, raising their hands in recognition that whatever rigours lie ahead, at least they are not alone, nor will be left alone until the last mother is left standing.

As our father pulls in under a tree not yet taken, there is Mr Mylrea, moving along the creek without his shirt. In his ordinary life Mr Mylrea is a vet, but on holiday he's clearly an altogether different creature. Emerging from the creek where he has been putting the milk, he is to me like a Time Measurer, an insect of fresh water. No more than an average imagination is required to see him and his extraordinarily long limbs steadily walking among the shady dapples of some creek weed. Against the grand backdrop of Mt Barney his colour is pale tan and we all like him immensely, not only because of our parents' affection for him but also for his tendency to really look at us as he says hello. I like his hairy arms and the way he greets me with the cheerfulness of sound I imagine a water insect would make, with something of creek breezes in there even though his voice is deep. Mr Fitzsimmons is nearby, his patchwork shorts shabbier than ever and my longing to have a piece of my clothing sewn in as part of a pocket still not realised. The Mylrea children are hovering around their mother who already, it would seem, has begun to distribute food and who therefore is possibly even more wonderful than her husband. If she had wings she'd scoot across the water at a million miles an hour, her colours suddenly clear and glinting in the light coming down through the she-oaks. Her hot chocolate sauce with raisins remains in my mind as the ultimate camping mystery. How and where would she prepare it? A cauldron full enough to ensure every camping child a dollop on top of their share of tinned Christmas pudding.

'Go and say hello,' says our mother but of course we don't. This would be too strange and too immediate. We have to watch the other children for a while, stunned by the sun on our backs and the remnant feelings of car sickness. 'Go and collect kindling, girls,' says our father and more than any other thing this is a good way of feeling well again. On my bare feet the grass is hot and yellow as I watch Yvonne breaking the bigger branches over her knee, or stepping onto the middle of them and pulling up one end. When I try to copy her the piece of branch pings on my foot, and I abandon the big bits, preferring even to this day to gather the thin, easy twigs as I go that are not swarming with ants.

I have never viewed the putting up of the tent with anything other than a sense of unassailable dread and this time is no exception. A wind always comes up. Just as the canvas is lifted off the ground and Greg Sneath is bending to his pole as if to hove it ten leagues deep, Karin's is literally pinged out of her hands and down it comes. I see it in a kind of slow motion and then it has knocked the side of my head and I am heading out through the canvas, dropping my pole which in turn hits Sonya and the whole construction begins to come down like a sail in a shipwreck.

'Yes!' says my father in a mood of reminiscence at a slide night, 'the tent poles did have an uncanny habit of falling on your head. And if I am permitted to say so, Gillian, you were a great caterwauler. If Karin or Yvonne got hit they'd sort of rub their heads and stoically keep going. But you would let out this kind of terrible wail. Then of course I'd be in strife and I'd have lost you as a pole holder.'

As a child, once the pain has subsided, it is quite worth the egg on the head to have escaped tent putting-up duties. Any manner of consolation may be offered by the mothers as well as permission from my own to go to the water. The air always seems afloat with the wings of black and orange butterflies and thistle seeds so thick the water is turning silver. High up in a tree over the water are the remains of a swing. The rope over any camping creek is invariably snapped off so high there isn't a chance of ever catching hold, not even with a running jump. I like to bend my face to the water to slurp in mouthfuls of Barney Creek. It tastes of cows and wild creatures, dead and living things, dragonflies, sun, eels in the darkest water under drowned logs and less definable things still.

ON THE NIGHT OF THE full moon, I wake up and can hear my family breathing. My little sister Sonya moans and flips a hand into the air, but even so I have the feeling of being alone underneath the tent, under the bull oak, whose needles are pointing towards me like dark fingers. The trees at Mt Barney are like people, even more so under starlight. I crawl from the tent, dragging my sleeping-bag with me to stand for a moment with my arms outstretched like a sapling hoop, my hands flipping up at the end. The hoop pines towards the fence are a solid block of black that I tiptoe towards in the direction of the fire.

It is the moon that has woken me, so like an eye in its strange circle of pink cloud. A moonlid, not moonlight, I think, blinking down at me. The clouds look as if they are part of a wind-torn ocean. Somewhere close by a cow bends low onto her knees before sinking closer to the ground. Mount Barney is not national park and I don't mind, not even the green slime that grows in the creek where the cattle come for water. I have a fondness for cows that I can never outgrow even if their presence is destroying the earth. I hear the cow's nose pull back with relief and the following sound like a sea monster of the deep. I also put my face down low to the earth. I blow on the coals and a piece of paper by the side of the fire ignites. As I keep blowing, red cinders fly off into the darkness and are so lost to sight that I quickly lower my shorts to squat in the grass. As I push out a few teaspoons of pee the crickets are singing in such a way it's as if they alone control how the stars are pulsing in the sky.

There is enough kindling to restart the fire. In the firelight a lump of petrified wood glows with a different kind of light. I see the slow lines of stone, but the time when this stone was living wood doesn't seem long ago to me. I completely burn a match and do my favourite trick, the one where you lick both sides of the soft part of each thumb before squashing the match between them. The imprint formed is like black tadpoles kissing, or punctuation marks.

After a while of crouching with my sleeping-bag around me like a cape, I take off the lid of a billy and commence my own secret feast. They are Mrs Mylrea's beans I've happened upon, with every now and then a lovely lump of sausage. I hope none of the rocks forming the circle around the fire will explode the way they sometimes do at night but I gauge my fire is nowhere near hot enough. I move a burning stick through the air, trying to write something in fast, looping, fiery letters, but the word is lost before I can finish. I draw a picture instead using charcoal and rock but soon am climbing back into my sleeping-bag, hopping and waddling across the land and back into place in the tent. The breathing has become deeper and as usual my father is snoring as if being pressed by a giant. I try to breathe in time with my family but they are all going at such different paces that in the end I must match my own with Sonya, who sleeps beside me.

When I wake up, my sisters and the Mylrea children are crouched about me, observing my face closely. 'What? What are you looking at?' I say, convinced I have turned into something odd overnight or that my face is covered in food or charcoal. Then even I see that I am in the wrong tent. Everyone is sure that I slept-walked myself into position at the end of Anthony's feet but to me it feels as if I've been inexplicably transferred here in the night.

No one can understand why suddenly, after laughing a little bit, I begin to cry. I don't even understand, when everyone's laughter is so fond and there is my mother at the mouth of the tent smiling and Mrs Mylrea kneeling across a jumble of bedclothes to offer a square of her very nice chocolate cake. Even the Time Measurer is watching me, his bushy eyebrows lifting in an expression of surprise when he catches my eye.

The tears are to do with the abrupt evaporation of the feeling of totally belonging. 'There, there, Gillian,' Mrs Mylrea is saying in my memory in a tone so tender I am aware of the other Gillian nearby becoming a bit fed up. 'Sit up now for some cake.' But I am crying my heart out for the cessation of an illusion which in a more perfect world would not be an illusion. In the communal living of the Naturalists Club camps the rigidity of nuclear families goes into limbo. Out under the sky each family simply can't be separate and alone. With the sharing of food and of the open toilets the fathers dig in the distance with an air of deliberate comedy, it is difficult to maintain any pretence of being a solo act.

Maybe in the Mylreas' tent, I cry in some secretly realised premonition that I will not experience this feeling of community and friendship again for people who are not my family until many years have passed. The feeling of belonging to a greater body of people than just my family will make a slow return in my thirties, but only after a most painful extrication from alcohol, and this only after living in a tent on a river, waiting for the day when more money comes through. It is the living outside which brings out a rapture for life that as I grew I let be buried by cities, addictions, bad marriages and the aftergloom of those things.

As I watch the laughter coming not just from the lips of the Mylreas but rising also in their bellies and eyes, I find that my body too is beginning to shake. Not with tears anymore but with happiness, as I explain how in the middle of the night I had my feast before hopping my way into the tent I felt sure was ours. I stand up in my sleeping-bag, demonstrating my movements and telling about the look of the moon, my midnight meal. The laughing pours out and for this moment we are *inter alios* and *in puris naturalibus*, hiding nothing. In the Mylreas' tent, the sleep still forming in our eyes and Mr Mylrea yet to do his morning shave using a billy and the mirror of his car, I do not want the day to go any further than this. We are some kind of *rara avis*, if not exactly of birds then birdlike, at least in the capering way we finally make our way out of the tent, our hair up on end, our funniest faces to the fore.

I am the last out of the Mylreas' tent but the wall of mist is still dense, the sunlight floating across the range like airborne honey. After the release of such deep emotion I feel that everything is hilarious, the bright rose-red mist above the creek, and my night art on the piece of petrified wood, that no one else notices except perhaps Mr P, sitting as he always does by the fire. He warms up the large fying pan on feet, at the same time scavenging bits of unburnt newspaper to read, his unruly yellow curls being clipped into obedience by his daughter, her mouth full of black bobby pins.

V DISJECTA MEMBRA [L.] *The Scattered Remains*

As we reach our double-figure-years – even Sonya is eleven – our mother's moods are less benign and in some subtle sense it's as if she has no choice but to punish us for not needing her in the same way, or for the ugly fashion in which our noses and our pimples are beginning to grow. We must eat brown and pink antibiotics against the fear of acne and steer clear of peanut butter and chocolate. The camping days seem so long ago that when the old slides are fished out one night to amuse our visiting grandma, it's hard to believe we are that happy group of four, cleaning our teeth on a rock near a river, the hair on our heads standing out like we're mops.

My nose which used to be an unnoticeable part of my face begins to shoot out as if it's part of a tree. I am turning into some kind of latter-day Pinocchio but staring in the mirror does anything but help. Our mother gets a job and people who could never be Naturalists Club campers come to parties at our house. In the prevailing atmosphere of disturbance, camping seems out of the question, so in the late seventies a decision is made to go back to the mountain lodge at Binna Burra. The lodge was built in the thirties for bushwalkers and nature lovers, and sometimes I believe that I only married my first husband due to the strong resemblance his house and garden bore to this childhood place. No sooner did I first step into my schoolteacher's garden, than some sense of recognition was forming in my mind and I understood completely Dylan Thomas's 'Fern Hill'. *Time held me green and dying/Though I sang in my chains like the sea.*

The air of Binna Burra excites our mother so much we all feel a rising hope that happiness can be recaptured. Our mother unwinds the windows to let in cool air laden with the smell of earth. Just as on every other holiday here, she exhorts us to breathe it in and when I do I feel as if the rapturous calls of currawongs are also slipping through the membranes of my skin, and that perhaps this is the way lyrebirds take in the songs of other birds. Do the birds know how lovely they sound? I wonder, their voices channelling up through the narrow space between Binna Burra's old cabins. If I tip back my throat and open my mouth will notes move through my lips like the last light on water?

Still without monthly blood and barely without breasts, at the beginning of the new school year I'll meet the teacher who will become my husband. It is his cottage I am sure that makes me feel so safe and cosy, hidden behind an ancient garden wound through with paths. His house and garden could be transplanted intact to Binna Burra and appear as one of the honeymoon cabins, and he one of its kind but less energetic guests; just like the businessman, there for food and reasons other than walking.

Although on the final family visit, Binna Burra lodge is not quite the same, it seems at first to be the salve my family is needing. We pile out of the car, glad that the bush turkeys are still roaming around near the dining room, even if the reading room with its wonderful mix of old books and chairs ancient enough to nearly swallow a beetle-shaped child has been turned into a room for games. Old Dick's presence is some kind of consolation. He's been coming to Binna Burra since its earliest days and tells us about the timber for the cabins being pulled out of the mountain with bullocks and much bloody swearing.

Our cabin is reached via steep rock steps and Sonya and I tear ahead in order that we might have the best choice of the four beds. Is it the solid sense of the timber slabs we run alongside that feeds us with energy greater than any that could be given by sugar or sustenance? Some essence of forest seems to convey itelf as we sleep in beds tucked down so tight I long always to encounter that exact feeling again; to find myself waking on a solid single bed, a pink-and-green rose quilt near my face smelling not so much of cloth as of knurly walls.

I let the treasures of each day's walk accumulate until just before the drive home when I must return leaf skeletons, a bush turkey's tail feather, the spent skins of spiders, a fungus that looks exactly like a penis in a petticoat, and a stone of such smoothness my father says that giant rivers must once have flowed across the land. My parents are so adamant about adhering to national park rules that they won't even let me take home a frog poo full of the magical colours of insect armour, which I have found on the lower Ballanjui Track. Yvonne sneers and will not hold it to her eye as I suggest in order to see its kaleidoscopic glints. She has turned so moody that instead of coming on walks she stays behind for the morning tea and scones put out for the old and the disabled at ten o'clock each day.

Many would say I am too young to notice the likeness of a fungus to a penis but the likeness is blindingly obvious and clearer to recall than the businessman's face.

I meet him one morning on the Blindman's Senses Track before breakfast. Mist is feathering off the top of Egg Rock in the Numinbah Valley. I smell his wallet and leather shoes first as I walk along with my eyes shut, one hand on the rope guide. Even pretending to be blind is daunting. At every post I stop to run my fingers over the freezing metal of braille explanation sheets which suggest to blind people they stretch their hands out to touch smooth or rough bark, or pause to hear the chitting of the little log-runner bird.

Underneath my arm is a smell like a snapped twig. It is at this moment, my shirt pulled up as I try to locate a marching ant, that I see the businessman watching me from the seat. I know at once that he isn't blind, due to the intensity of his look. He must be transfixed by my bones, for my breasts are no more than two buds pushing up under my flesh. 'Skinnyguts,' my mother often says to me, examining me sometimes in a way that makes me feel like poor Hansel being fattened up for the witch's dinner.

I know too that the businessman's a different kind of old man to Dick whose lap we can lean against without thought, and that unlike Dick he doesn't seem to have been grown in a beech forest. His shoes are slip-ons, not walking boots, and he is quite fat, as if walking is not really a part of his life. Yet still, when he pats the bench, I decide that I will sit there with him for a while, as if he is a blind man to whom you should be kind. I think of the caramel-coloured dog for the blind, the slot in his head for donations, that I used to like to stroke when I was little. The businessman sits on a log seat, a newspaper under his trousers to stop them getting damp, and when he sees I will sit down he stands up, moves his camera and spreads some of the newspaper out to my section of the seat.

I sit picking away at a peeling section of my arm, waiting for the breakfast bell. In front of us the land drops steeply. It is not rainforest we are sitting in front of but land that has been burnt and cleared. There are some tall gum trees and we're sitting so close to the lodge above us that I can hear the cook rattling the bacon pan. As I work systematically to peel my arm, the businessman jangles coins in his pocket. 'Look,' he says, handing me a foreign coin with a hole in it, 'you can have that if you like.' I examine it for a moment before holding it to my eye as if it is a lens. I put the coin in my jeans pocket and continue to peel my old suntan down from the roundest part of my upper arm. The closer to my elbow I get, the thinner and more tearable is the skin, and the more difficult it is to free a really good-sized piece.

The track to our left has so many spiders that have threaded lines up from the ground into gum trees it's as if they have guyed a tall tent somewhere up there in the sky. Did I know, the businessman asks me, that the man whom the plateau is named after, Lord Lamington, also gave his name to the chocolate- and coconut-covered cakes?

As a fact in exchange, I tell him that the river of my town rises in these ranges.

'We used to come here with Mother, oh at least once a year,' he tells me. 'Father never cared for the walks but we did them all with Mother. She only died a fortnight ago. I have her photo somewhere.' His eyes fill with tears. 'My sister and I are going to scatter her ashes today. But we're having a bit of disagreement about where. Here or at O'Reilly's.' I feel such a rush of pity, natural to any child aunt, that it seems to me now that from the first, desire has always mixed itself up in me with the hope of being able to console someone's sorrow. Although the skin of his throat is as baggy as the socks around my ankles it is my desire both sexual and helpful which somehow connects me to him.

I smile when he asks could he have a turn at peeling my arm. His hands are too soft and fat for the task and he laughs, declaring that he has lost the knack. I don't want him to stop though, for fat or not his fingers prompt shivery sensations in and around each bone of my body. Finally he takes hold of a good piece and manages to get a small circle. The tearing sound of my skin is more fragile than any I have ever heard and he seems to hear it too, for he stops, breaks it off as if it is stickytape on a roll, and holds the skin that was only a dead part of me anyway up to the light.

Placing my patch of skin on the bench between us he says it is as delicate as the silk spun by certain types of spiders. This silk, he says, is neither for climbing nor snaring but serves to hold the substance which the male spider draws into his front legs to later put into the female spider to create babies. He tells me that the silk mats may be found sometimes, abandoned in the way of birds' nests, but rarely recognised. He's not wrong in deciding that I'm the kind of girl interested in such things, for in my nature collection at home is the old birthing purse of a huntsman spider, the silk so harsh after the babies have hatched that anybody who didn't know would think it to be a rather tough bit of paper. For a moment I look into the businessman's sleepy eye with the pupil and iris floating up to show the eyeball.

Then he comments that I remind him of a heifer on sandstone country, as if he could tell from the feeling of my skin alone on what kind of land I'm growing.

'Ah,' he says next, 'here's my sister.' His sister appears from the other end of the trail looking more than anything else like a walking rug. Although she isn't blind either, she walks with one hand on the rope, with an air of uncertainty, ducking underneath the spiderwebs. Her dress is so handmade and heavy I imagine that if it did rain, the weight of it would waterlog her beyond movement. 'I was just showing Gillian a picture of Mother.' I jump, because I haven't told him my name.

He waves his hand, pleased by my surprise. 'I heard it the other evening. Over dinner,' he says. 'Your family had come in from the Coomera Circuit.'

Unlike the businessman his sister is not very friendly. She appears to glare at me, so that I leave the damp bench for the blind then, saying a polite goodbye and leaving my skin behind. What insect or what bird, I wonder, will carry away my skin for a meal? Or will the businessman collect it like a kind of nature specimen? Will he stick it down beside other interesting objects found on this trip, labelling my main physical characteristics and the quality of my voice? I'm making a fairly fast getaway when he calls to ask if he can take my photograph. He takes two pictures with the bush turkeys stabbing away behind me like a circle of sewing machines at the grass.

I have barely spent ten minutes in the businessman's company but when I reach the breakfast room where my sisters are already sitting, everything, even the cream porridge bowl rimmed with green and the lyrebird symbol, is different. I feel the same kind of stillness I do in looking at green huntsman's eggs: I know they are about to erupt with life, but for the moment of my gaze they are as still as miniature green grapes inside their immaculate and perfectly white egg-sac. Everyone's eating as if there's no tomorrow but my food seems to be reaching my lips in slow motion. I keep glancing at the door to see if he will come in for breakfast too, but in fact I never see the businessman again.

He returns only in the night, part of the tiger-snake-in-the-library dream. Or he comes glancing into my mind decades on as I crouch in long grass behind the schoolteacher's house, watching a spider that looks like a drip of metal moving on silver legs. I think of him with a degree of wonder as meditation descends over me in my thirties like a calm veil. However did he or anybody else affect my body so powerfully?

At Binna Burra I imagine the businessman lifting up one of my summer dresses two dozen times over. The businessman and the teacher smell not of bushwalks, grass sap or smoke, and under my reluctant but curious fingers their trousers are not soft to the touch in the way I imagine the shorts of a Naturalists Club boy's would have been – cotton – thinned by the sun and the wind. My whole life might have been different had the first person I kissed been a Naturalists Club boy or a Naturalists Club girl, with a lean, unconstipated belly. No guilt in such a kiss, just skin and salty hair and lips split with sunburn.

As the last days of the last Binna Burra family holiday go by, I keep remembering the smell of the businessman. Instead of paying attention to the sphagnum moss like little green feathers on wet rocks, or to the curves of strangler figs, I am sniffing the air, searching for the scent of a wallet containing the currency of different countries. Even as I am enjoying my family's presence at a waterfall pool I realise I would also like to be swimming without my family, with a man who is not our father taking the snapshots. Our father and mother take off their clothes for a quick dip and although we've seen their bodies each day for all of our lives, we all avert our eyes, wishing they would bring swimmers. Huddled over the chocolate my mother says will be the ruin of my complexion, I feel more stranded than the day I suffered vertigo at Girraween but there is no one this time who can rescue me from my invisible fears. I peer into deep crevices, hoping to sight a blue and white Lamington yabbie. Only the cool air comes back to me, sad and dark and with a little whiff of something like Stockholm tar from the moss – a healing sting.

I stop by a tree that stands to one side of the path like a huge mother, her legs apart. I walk through into the hollow between, as if by one sure step I can again find myself in a kind of womb, dark and steady with supporting life. A long time ago the tree has been burnt. Inside is warmer than the outside air. I look up thinking this must be what it is like to be blind, this kind of blackness.

When I slip back out, my family has disappeared and although I hear no sound of them up ahead, the currawongs sound slower and for the first time ever a note of despair lies somewhere in their song. I hurry on, not stopping to pick up skeleton leaves as fine as dress gauze. My boots strike a hardness like bronze but it is tree roots, burnished by decades of walkers. I run in fear that darkness will fall and that in the fading light I'll plunge off the side of the track, out of the forest and into the farmlands that lie far below, never to be found by my family again.

Back in the cabin where the wall of mist makes seeing anything but the nearest tree impossible, I draw a heart on the window. I have no initials to place in there apart from BM. If I'd met him on a beach and not above a forest, the reality of flesh might have immediately put halt to the fantasy, but being a cool morning he was hidden in woollen trousers. If only the day of seeing the middens with my schoolteacher had been sunny. Maybe then, upon seeing their shape, their breasts bigger than my own, the black hair crossing them, I would have turned away and not towards their own loneliness. Then the twin desires – in them to make love to a child, in me to choose someone much older – would have been thwarted before they could properly begin.

Or if only the schoolteacher had lived in a house less beautiful, without a pointed roof. If only he hadn't been able to tell stories as alluring as fairy tales. The schoolteacher, whom I meet only weeks after the last Binna Burra holiday, has a house like the gingerbread cottage of Hansel and Gretel, promising happiness and safety, cosy cups of hot chocolate and the high, holiday feeling of small windy paths disappearing into leaf litter and soil, leaf-coloured birds flitting about like little ghosts.

When he eventually moves his body into my own, when at last I am old enough and far enough away from home, I'm still thinking of the businessman and of Binna Burra. I'm thinking of the roots of Lamington Plateau figs, stronger looking than bone, and of how higher up, towards the light, the fig branches appear to melt over the host tree, absorbing and finally destroying the host. I feel my schoolteacher melting over my body. 'You give me life,' is his most commonly expressed feeling. In my quest to stay a child I've chosen this, and even though he sometimes tells me to speak in a bigger voice, the schoolteacher will do his level best to allow me never to grow up.

VI ANCIEN RÉGIME [F.]   *The Old Order*

You would have to come to a slide night to really see us. I can't think of any other act or memory that captures the way the old black and white tents are billowing in my mind, behind the silvery background. Or how the children are standing knee-deep in the creek, only freshly arrived, still hugging the flanks of their sisters or brothers, the family clumps yet to dissolve.

At the slide night, organised in the kind of last-minute frenzy in which weekend expeditions used to be, we look at the slides as best we may. Due to a shortage of chairs in the farmhouse, I sit on my blue, yellow and crimson cushion next to the temperamental projector and crooked towers of half-empty slide boxes, and as the evening progresses I can feel travelling up and down my spine, into my feet and along my legs, the same deep tingling sensations meditation can bring.

Nothing is quite so exposing as a slide night and only friends with a deep and abiding love of the family and its idiosyncrasies are ever allowed along. I couldn't imagine one where only beautiful pictures are shown; it is the imperfections that make me smile with fondness. I love the slide of Mrs Mylrea, on what might be day four or five of an Easter camp. Children are capering around her like dogs around a bag of bones. I think it is Easter eggs she has in her hand, or something equally worth all the attention. Her hair is so thinned with the grease of no shampoos that we can all see, twenty-five years on, her vulnerable white scalp, the look of helpless pleasure on her tired face as her son leaps into the air, exhorting her with a wild grin for the last egg.

On slide nights at the farm, I am the organising aunt and I am the child aunt. To simply be, watching slides, is quite easy, enjoying the fond laughter of my family. Look, we are happy there, hopping along a creek full of round rocks and disintegrating logs, our heads held at the most hopeful of angles, no inkling then that one day the slide will be so old and the scene so removed it will reappear to us like some faded bible illustration, enlarged and cast upon the wall.

'Slow down, slow down,' the rest of the family say as I move the slide cartridge in and out. But the mistake with old projectors and slides fattened with age is to go slowly, and the machine jams abruptly on a picture of the white Peugeot station wagon that carries us like a wingless chariot to most of the holidays of childhood.

As I try to fix the projector our father proceeds to relate the familiar story of how one weekend he had to leave us all, except for Sonya who wasn't yet born, in the new car. Karin takes over the story and then Yvonne, as if it is one of the Carry-on Stories that were always a part of Naturalists Club campfires.

Bored with waiting in the car and grumpy that the usual ploy of beeping the car horn hadn't yet brought out the figure of our father, Yvonne's eyes landed on the screwdriver on the back seat. With initially worried then happy encouragement from Karin, Yvonne began to jab the screwdriver into the upholstery. So enticing was the pop of air and leather that Karin also had to have a turn. 'The only time we ever got a smack,' they tell their own children with delight.

The nieces and nephews pour from the room in good humour following this unlikely tale to do the yearly treasure hunt, so that when I give the projector a good shake and a sharp slap, no children are left as it whirrs back into action.

More than ever in the next slide, my appearance is that of a monkey astronaut – my haircut with the severe lines of a small space helmet. And the expression on my four- or five-year-old's face is similarly tragic, as though I know I am going to be shot forth into unchartered space. If I look and listen hard enough, my old/young monkey face says to me, then the understanding about childhood that I never stop seeking will at last be clear.

When watching old slides, I want to say to my sisters who've also vanished from the room, think of lichen on a rock. Although you are focused on something very intricate and tiny, if you look for long enough you begin to feel that you may actually be staring into the secret of galaxies and atmospheres or a tiny depiction of the Milky Way, put down on a piece of sandstone so purple it is nearly black, for your contemplation alone. *Vipassana*. I like to utter the ancient Pali word aloud. *To see things as they really are.* Like a shell pressed into my ear, the name of the meditation I practise fills me with feelings of despair, longing and hope. I know as little Pali as I do Latin but the dictionaries on my desk make me dream that one day there'll be more time for learning. Oh *Glochidian ferdinandi* – the majestic roll of the words under the yellow cheese tree of that name as I collect their seeds which are so temperamental to germinate.

Sometimes it seems to me that my writing has been nothing more than a long in-memorium notice and always to the memory of childhood. Or hasn't it always been a kind of meditation, wherein the old memories and fresh images rise up to be observed as the moving pen crosses the white page, only to be finished with once the writing is over, the final moment of detachment occurring once the words are published? Or perhaps it has been nothing more than reaction after reaction after reaction, with little distance from the range of emotions that have inspired the creative act in the first place.

Perhaps like the other old addictions, writing too might pass, this need to try to fasten everything down in a glut of images. One day I might go walking without the notebook always in my pocket. I imagine letting go all of my images, collected like precious stones and hoarded against some more difficult day. Why labour anymore over the story of the Parisian canary? Not in twenty or twenty hundred pages can I ever hope to produce the perfection of the little native mouse who is obviously hoping to set up home in my van too, whom I don't want to kill even if she does choose to have her babies behind the shelf for unread books.

Sitting at my desk I pick up the largest of my crab's claws. I can say that the colours darken as they turn around each joint, becoming as thick as old paint mixed by the miniature monkeys of ancient Chinese scholars, or that its look is of dried blood on white china. I can seek for any number of words in a dictionary that's far larger than the *Collins Gem* and still feel that I'm failing. The closer the stare, the more I see – fragments of gold in between the red so that it appears to be illuminating before my eyes, or turning into a detail from an Indian miniature of Arjuna and Krishna going to war, painted with a one-hair brush in Rajasthan, hundreds of years ago for a hoity prince. I move the claw in the air before my pen and hear how the crab might once have sounded, crossing from rocks into water.

Maybe what I have really meant by the term child aunt is child who might write.

The three child aunts whom I see at such regular intervals through the year that I have the corner shop man tricked into believing they're my own are the most likely ones to be writerly. These are the children who recall their dreams as the porridge is being stirred, who see images where no one else can. 'Look!' yells a child aunt swimming with me to the rock where the skinks live. 'A woman in the sky. There's her bum. She's twisting round!'

They are letter-writers and readers. They dog-ear pages of my old childhood books and dive fully clothed into the floodwater streaming over the grasses under my camp. There is something frank and unflinching in their appraisal of life. Their tolerance to pain is high as they pierce each other's ears using ice, dental floss and a sewing needle.

The child aunts seem to have the frightening eyes of cameras, missing nothing, but they like to mother baby animals and are adept at crafts. A child aunt may appear to have an air of absence, an air of worry, trying to turn some spare wool into coats for the baby rats saved from the bulldozer, but really she's missing nothing, knitting needles poised, her familially large ears alert to the gossip. It is the child aunt, turning a secretive gaze into the corners of windows or the eyes of animals, who sees reflected the things not meant to be sighted.

A few years ago, when my family was beset by problems, a sister, counter-accusing me on another matter altogether, said that my writing had been like a spider at my family's neck, sucking it dry. To be a writer for me has been to be a scavenger, more hyena than spider really, my good memory painstakingly, consciously and unconsciously, storing up all that I have seen and heard. People tell me their dangerous stories and I want to put some kind of nerve block in place, some barricade that will stop any detail seeping into my own life and fiction, and in this way never be accused again.

I think of my only living aunt and of how my writing has filled her with fear; how my writing has lost her to me. She never sends her long green letters anymore, bursting with descriptions of birds, pears or Western Australian flowers, for fear of some detail popping up in a book. When I hear the aunt bird calling tears of regret can sting my eyes. I fill the small vase she sent me for my fifth birthday with tulip-wood pods and decide to photograph this as a card I can post, seeking to make amends.

The cowrie shell procession I make along my desk is like a parade of colours of all the eyes I have ever known, flecked and soulful, or the ancient blue of the very old or very young. I can see the eyes of my sisters and their children, the hazy marks, the rings of aquamarine. I can pick up a grey one remembering this was the kind of colour in my favourite schoolteacher's eye.

Ever since my sisters began to give birth to my surrogate children I've been taking photographs and they are always holiday photographs, with that particular holiday presence, of solemnity and glee, or a stillness so weighted in the children's faces it is as if they have nothing more to learn and will shortly be leaving the earth, fully enlightened.

I place the photographs with great care into the kind of old-fashioned albums that have dark cardboard just one particular shade of grey, that I can only buy from a shop in Sydney. The dividing paper is marked in spiderweb patterns and stops the nephews' faces sticking to the nieces' as the years go by.

Photographs were my first kind of meditation – far sooner than any story I tried to write. I used to annoy my schoolteacher, who had by then become my husband, sitting late into the night, gazing at the face of this baby on her mother's knee in the middle of the creek at Diggers, or that nephew with seasponge cups over his hands like mittens. I used to bore his friends too, carrying the aunt album everywhere with me and anticipating that they too would like to pore over the album at the same slow pace. My schoolteacher thought my obsession indicated a desire for children of our own but this desire for me has remained like a shadow on a tent wall, only ever half glimpsed. I hear he is a father now and think he must be a good one, his camera always at the ready, his long hands good with nappy pins and rattly toys. His Binna Burra garden would make a fine backdrop for family photos, the baby laughing as his father pushes the self-timer button and hurtles towards the rose bushes to make it into position in time.

I look at photographs searching for wider patterns and connections. I search for early signs of animosities between sisters who refuse to speak to each other, reaching back into the earliest albums put together by my mother, great-grandmother and great-aunt Noel.

'How old do we seem?' my sisters and I can be heard asking the nieces and nephews, with a wistful air, knowing it to be much older than we feel. We hope they can still see the child's shyness as opposed to the shyness of an adult, lying open in our faces at certain moments of hesitation and regret. No one ever calls me aunt, though it is the role in life in which I most revel.

THE SMELL OF WOODSMOKE IS deep in the pores of my writing hand and every now and then I take a pause from the page to smell this, and the effect isn't unlike some elixir of youth.

Only when the nieces, nephews and three child aunts come to stay at camp with me, setting up in smaller tents behind my larger one near the caravan, do the sensations of holidays make a dramatic return.

They say, 'Look, Gillian!' At the small insect with green and white stripes like an onion, the turtle on the rock, the dog eating a river crab, or B's tower of kindling, five feet high now on the left-hand side of the cooking fire.

Whether or not they see, down by the swimming rock, how light runs across water into their skin and out again, I have never asked. B's rescuing insects with a stick and the others are being as gluttonous as calves on buckets full of mangoes, before leaping into the river to wash the stickiness away. In the company of the children I'm sure that I've been readmitted to some earthly paradise. They are still before the age of plucking, pulling, picking, preening, but I can feel the precariousness of time left. The day will come when it won't be possible to swim without clothes, and I know I'm not imagining the way that the oldest child aunt in particular has begun to look in horror at hairs on her aunt where she perceives hairs should not really grow.

The exact moment of expulsion from any paradise is as hard to pinpoint as the position of mosquitoes flying around the light of my desk. They are poised, definite, delicate, but the moment I try to usher them out of my door they are no longer there. Just for one night I try to follow the precept about not killing any living thing. I let the mosquitoes feast on until another sensation of old holidays is unexpectedly reached. Itchiness. They bite through the tough elbow skin the way mosquitoes always used to and land lightly over the knuckles of my fingers, until abandoning all attempts at equanimity I scratch the bites as a child always does, and they bleed.

Like a heifer on sandstone country, said the businessman, as if he could understand all those years ago the kind of country to which I would always return.

Cows that never have calves don't usually have long lives but I have the grace of having been turned into an aunt. I'm passing through the childbearing years on sandstone country, and though a child with a high forehead like a calf sometimes appears in a meditation, she is quickly gone.

The cows around my camp and caravan move like a black and white jigsaw puzzle of which I seem a part, across the green river flats and down to the high tide for a drink. Up close it is as if smaller pieces of black, pink and white puzzle make up their wet, sweet smelling noses. Sometimes I fall asleep on the cushion where I meditate and it is only a millipede crawling over my foot, or a calf walking underneath a rusty line of Tibetan prayer bells that makes me sit upright, trying to concentrate again on the great knot of pain that begins to settle in my right shoulder.

In the children's tents the conversation and laughter is reaching a crescendo and then without warning, soon after dark, sleep is upon them, as if a spell has been cast. My handwriting is so small and erratic no other eyes except my own could ever make out the early drafts, the scribbled images, the corrections made on the walls like a builder's calculations. Photographs will always be more easily accessible. Even the gaps in the albums are significant, being those stolen by sisters who feel that in this or in that image must lie some inkling of their inner essence. We always cherish most what is lost. There is a power in the absence of my favourite correspondent's letters from my mailbox and greater accretions of meaning around his letters from earlier years. Did I ever care so tenderly for the aunt's letters before she asked me to post them back across Australia, never to be seen by my eyes again?

The time is just after the hour when once I would've had my final whiskey for the night that would knock me into a comalike sleep. I am not remotely tired, meditation having replenished in me that same childhood alertness, that feeling that there is not a moment to lose, and certainly not in sleep. My pen crosses the page as methodically as a copepod might an ocean, with steady oarlike movements.

The candle smells of fire. The pregnant mouse smells it too, darting out, her nose trembling. Fire I'm sure isn't the answer we're hoping to find. I balance a ruler with a knob of peanut butter and oats over a bucket, hoping that by tomorrow I'll have caught the mother-to-be.

Looking down at a closed photo album, or a piece of writing that has reached its natural end, I'm often reminded of the haiku poetry of Basho – his ability to capture leave-takings, his brevity. I think of a beach track emptied suddenly of children, who have reached the larger expanse of sand.

I copy a haiku from an old page of poems, unsure after all that it's a Basho. I use the writing twigs I enjoy so much, snapping them to form each letter on the floor.

THE TEMPLE BELL STOPS,

BUT THE SOUND KEEPS COMING OUT OF THE FLOWERS.

At some time in the night, on her way to the bucket that will carry her to safety, the mouse knocks against the twigs in such a way that they still make a kind of sense. Captured next morning, she holds her paws to her face in the position of praying and trembles as if gripped by fever as well as fear.

I drive with the children to an abandoned shed to let her go. It is a little bit like allowing a caught fish its freedom, only it's into grass not water she disappears. For a moment the grass lifts as if by a puff of breath and then not even a child's eye can locate her position. The shed roof reaches the sky like a sail tacking towards shore. We take leave of the mysteries of a small native mouse then, her grey tail tip just visible under a leaf pile. I remember the haiku she altered last night in my doorway:

THE TEMPLE BELL STOPS,

BUT THE SOUND Leeps COMING OUT OF THE   OWERS.

/   FL